COASTAL CREATURES

By
Robin Twiddy

BookLife
PUBLISHING

King's Lynn
Norfolk PE30 4LS

Printed in Malaysia.

A catalogue record for this book is available from the British Library.

ISBN: 978-1-78637-989-4

Written by:
Robin Twiddy

Edited by:
Madeline Tyler

Designed by:
Gareth Liddington

Photo credits:

Cover – donatas1205, Fotana, StockPhotosArt, Madlen, tropicdreams, Eric Isselee, 2 – Elise V, 4 – ShutterProductions,5 – GOLFX, Roland Magnusson, gopfaster, Komkrit Noenpoemplust, Andrey Eremin, maxpro, 6 – kryzhov, 7 – Polianskyl Igor, 8 – Sergey Uryadnikov, 9 – LouieLea, 10 – Michael Smith ITWP, 11 – Neophuket, 12 – Hans Viveen, 13 – Johnny Glese, 14 – C E Newman, 15 – oksana2010, WealthyLady, Nishlhama, 16 – jbutcher, 17 – Daolauong Kamkhom, 18 – Joanna K-V, Ingrid Pakats, MG Image and design, Tanya Ustenko, 20 – Martin Prochazkacz, 21 – Khalril Azhar Junos, 22 – Vanatchanan, 23 – FILINdesign, Prokhorovich.

Images are courtesy of Shutterstock.com. With thanks to Getty Images, Thinkstock Photo and iStockphoto.

CONTENTS

Words that look like this can be found in the glossary on page 24.

LET'S EXPLORE

WELCOME, COAST EXPLORER!

Today, we will be looking for coastal and marine creatures. By exploring different coastlines, you will find different coastal creatures.

GRAB YOUR EQUIPMENT

A budding coast explorer will need:

Notebook and pencil

Bucket

Binoculars

Camera

Waterproofs

EXPLORER SAFETY

Being a coast explorer is very exciting, but it can be dangerous if you do not follow the rules of the coast.

!

WHEN YOU SEE THIS SYMBOL, IT MEANS THAT THERE IS SOMETHING DANGEROUS NEARBY. THE DANGER WARNING WILL TELL YOU HOW TO STAY SAFE.

Always make sure that you know where an adult is when you are at the coast. You should also make sure that you always know when the tide is coming in and going out.

SEALS

Blubber keeps seals warm in cold waters.

Seals are marine mammals and can be found in most waters around the world, although they prefer colder water. Seals have a thick layer of fat called blubber.

Seals can often be found in large groups on rocks or sandbanks. You should use your binoculars to get a closer look without disturbing them.

SEALS HAVE BEEN KNOWN TO BITE. KEEP YOUR DISTANCE.

Seals can grow anywhere from one metre to five metres long.

SEA TURTLES

There are seven species of sea turtle and nearly all of them are endangered. Sea turtles live in the ocean but they need to come to the surface to breathe air.

Sea turtles live in almost every ocean in the world. They can be found nesting on tropical and subtropical beaches. If you see turtles on a beach, do not get too close.

HARBOUR PORPOISES

Groups of porpoises are called pods.

Harbour porpoises can be found swimming very close to the shore. You can get a good view of them if you take a trip out on a boat to their feeding grounds.

Find an area where harbour porpoises have been spotted before. Watch the water with your binoculars. If they are around, you might spot their fins poking out of the water.

Harbour porpoises are usually found in cool waters, such as those off the coast of the UK.

SHELLFISH

The coast is a great place to find shellfish. Shellfish are invertebrates that live in hard shells. Lots of coastal creatures eat shellfish, and so do lots of people.

You can forage for shellfish on the beach. This means that you can take them home and cook them to eat. Here are some types of shellfish that people collect on the beach.

Mussels

Clams

Cockles

Make sure that an adult prepares and cooks them for you.

HERMIT CRABS

Have you ever seen a shell crawling across the sand at the beach? Look very closely next time because it could be a hermit crab.

Hermit crabs have soft bodies that they protect by curling up inside borrowed shells they find. When they grow bigger, they will leave that shell to find a bigger one.

Hermit crabs have been known to make homes in litter such as plastic bottles and cans, but shells make the best homes.

JELLYFISH

Jellyfish are not very good swimmers. They rely on the <u>currents</u> of the ocean to move around, but this can lead to them being left on the beach when the tide goes out.

NEVER TOUCH A JELLYFISH. EVEN VERY SMALL JELLYFISH CAN STING.

Lion's mane jellyfish on a beach

A coast explorer should learn to identify different types of jellyfish. Here are a few common types.

Moon jellyfish: clear with four pink rings, sting might prickle

Compass jellyfish: compass-like markings, painful sting

Blue jellyfish: small, blue or purple in colour, painful sting

SHARKS

Basking sharks can be found around the coast of the UK in the summer months. They feed on plankton.

There are many types of shark. Some are big. Some are small. Some, such as the basking shark, do not have teeth. Some sharks live along coastlines and some just visit.

Shark egg cases can often be found on the beach. They tell us that there is a type of shark living in the waters nearby.

There are many websites that you can use to identify egg cases.

SOME SHARKS CAN BE VERY DANGEROUS. DO NOT SWIM IN AREAS THAT ARE KNOWN TO HAVE DANGEROUS SHARKS.

KEEPING NOTES

There are so many amazing things to see along the coast. We cannot take all of the things we find home with us.

Keeping notes in your notebook will help you to remember what you saw.

What have you seen at the coast? Have you found any unusual creatures? Were there egg cases on the beach?

GLOSSARY

currents	constant movements of sea water in a certain direction
endangered	when a species of animal is in danger of going extinct
forage	to search for food
identify	spot or recognise
invertebrates	animals without a backbone
mammals	animals that are warm blooded, have a backbone and produce milk to feed their children
marine	things relating to the ocean
nesting	making a nest to have young in
plankton	a collection of tiny creatures and plants that float together in a body of water
shore	the land next to an ocean, sea, river or lake
subtropical	to do with areas that are close to tropical areas
tide	the movement of the ocean towards and away from land
tropical	to do with the part of the world that is most hot and humid

INDEX